A Color & Learn Guide for Kids

How to Care for Your CAT

Janet Skiles

DOVER PUBLICATIONS, INC.
Mineola, New York

NOTE

Cats are a lot of fun to play with and have as pets, but they do need care and attention from you to remain happy and healthy. In this coloring book are tips on how to keep your cat safe, what to do when you bring a new kitten home, how to "cat proof" your home, and more. You can color the pages with crayons, pencils, or markers. There is also a connect-the-dots puzzle on page 29 and a chart to keep track of your daily kitty care on page 30.

Bibliographical Note

How to Care for Your Cat: A Color & Learn Guide for Kids is a new work, first published by Dover Publications, Inc., in 2011.

International Standard Book Number

ISBN-13: 978-0-486-48148-7
ISBN-10: 0-486-48148-4

Manufactured in the United States by Courier Corporation
48148402
www.doverpublications.com

You can adopt a kitten or cat from a local animal shelter or a pet shop. Be sure to choose the best match for your lifestyle. Kittens are very active and older cats are more laid back and love to just curl up in your lap.

Your new companion will need to visit the veterinarian
(pet doctor) for vaccinations and a check-up. The veterinarian
will tell you everything you need to know
about keeping your pet healthy.

Sometimes cats can wander off and get lost. Make sure your cat has a collar with an identification tag attached to it. The tag should have your address and phone number on it. This way if somebody finds your cat they will be able to find you.

Kittens are very curious and can sometimes get in trouble when roaming around a new home. Make sure you have a nice, safe area set aside for your new kitten. Add a soft, fluffy bed and your new arrival will feel right at home!

4

Cats need plenty of fresh food and water. When you first bring your cat home make sure you buy the same food she was used to eating, otherwise she could get an upset stomach. You can switch her food over to your brand a little at a time.

Your cat's litter box should be kept clean at all times. Cats can be fussy and don't like dirty litter boxes. You should have at least one litter box on each level of your home, especially if you have a young kitten or an older cat.

Kittens love to have fun, so make sure you have plenty of
safe toys on hand for him to play with including little
plush toys and balls. Also, kittens love to climb on things,
so get him a scratching post.

Cats need to have a scratching post in the house. They use the post for climbing, stretching, and to remove the outer layer of their nails to keep them sharp. Scratching posts come in all different shapes and sizes.

When picking up your cat, place one hand under her chest right behind his front legs, then place your other hand under his back legs and lift him up holding him close to your body. Never pick your cat up by the scruff of the neck!

Keep your cat's coat in good condition with regular brushing
sessions. Short-haired cats need brushing once a week;
long-haired cats should be brushed once a day.
After you are done, give your cat a treat!

Once your new kitten is used to all her new surroundings, you can let her start to explore the rest of the house. Make sure you keep an eye on her so she doesn't wind up in trouble.

To keep your cat safe you need to think like a cat! Get down on the floor and look around for small objects he could choke on, electrical wires he might want to chew, or anything else that could be dangerous for a curious cat.

Cats can easily choke on small items such as rubber bands,
paper clips, broken balloons, thumb tacks, Christmas tree tinsel,
and ribbons. They can also get their heads stuck in the handles
of plastic bags and choke, so store them away in a cabinet.

Make sure that all cords for your curtains and blinds are tied
up high out of reach and out of sight of your kitten.
Electrical cords can be fastened together and pulled up
so they are not laying on the floor.

Curious cats like to explore by jumping up on things like furniture. Sometimes this can get them into trouble. Especially when they jump on a table and knock over a valuable treasure. So keep anything breakable off your tables.

Until your kitten is trained to use a scratching post,
you should cover your couches and chairs with some blankets.
This will protect your furniture from the claws of your
kitten and keep it clean.

A scratching post with a toy attached will give your kitten hours of fun climbing around and batting the toy. If you sprinkle a little catnip on the post, your cat will be even more attracted to it and will leave your furniture alone.

17

For your pet's safety, check to make sure the plants in your home are not poisonous. If they are poisonous, or if you are not sure, give them away. You can do your research at your local library or ask an adult to help you look it up on the Internet.

Cats love to play! They especially like to hide and jump out of paper grocery bags (make sure the handles are removed) and in cardboard boxes (have an adult check to see if there are any sharp staples in the boxes that could scratch your cat).

Chasing things is another activity that cats love. A favorite
cat toy is a stick with a string at the end that is tied to a
lightweight small toy. Move this around and watch your cat
jump, run, and attack the toy!

You must teach your kitten how to play nice. If he scratches, bites, or bats you with his paw, then stop playing and give him a "time out" by leaving the room. Never hit or punish your kitten!

A favorite activity for cats is hiding and ambushing your feet or ankles as you walk by. To avoid this, carry a small toy in your pocket and toss it before your cat goes after you. He will then chase the toy instead of you!

Indoor cats are healthier and live longer than cats that go outside. This is because they are not exposed to diseases, other animals, and cars. If you want to bring her outside, be safe and put a harness on her.

Nobody knows your cat better than you! If you see signs that he is not eating, or if he is acting strangely, then he will need to visit the veterinarian. A vet will examine him and tell you what to do to make him feel better.

When you need to travel with your cat in the car, be safe
and put her in a cat carrier. Make sure to secure the carrier
with a seat belt so it doesn't move around. Also, never leave
your cat in the car unattended!

Kittens love to cuddle! At night when you go to bed, don't be surprised if your kitten snuggles up with you.
Cats like to curl up on nice, soft blankets and will especially enjoy you being there, too!

Cats are wonderful companions! If you give your cat plenty of
love, petting, and praise, you will have a happy cat.
There's nothing better than a wonderful, purring cat
sleeping on your lap!

To take good care of your cat, bring him for yearly veterinarian
checkups, and play with him regularly.
This way, you will have a happy, healthy pet for many years.
Remember, you are your cat's best friend!

Follow the dots from 1 to 20 to see
who is trying to peek in the fish bowl.

29

Daily Kitty Care	Monday	Tuesday	Wednesday	Thursday	Friday	Saturday	Sunday
Love and praise kitty							
Feed kitty							
Give kitty water							
Clean litterbox							
Play with kitty							
Brush kitty							
Make sure dangerous objects are out of kitty's reach							
More love, petting and praise							